Social responsibility
We need more and realize less

Hans-Peter Hummel

Social responsibility

We need more and realize less

Bibliografische Information der Deutschen Nationalbibliothek:
Die Deutsche Nationalbibliothek verzeichnet diese Publikation in der Deutschen Nationalbibliografie; detaillierte bibliografische Daten sind im Internet über http://dnb.dnb.de abrufbar.

Illustration: Hans-Peter Hummel

Herstellung und Verlag: BoD – Books on Demand, Norderstedt

ISBN: 978-3-7448-2046-2

Introduction

We are social beings. We work together and spend a lot of our leisure time with other people. We need the contact and the interaction with other people.

We need each other. We are not a lot of "lone wolfs"[1], we need solidarity.

Today – and considerably more in the future – it is hardly possible to develop a major or even a brilliant invention alone without others.

We need a high degree of collaboration and the trend is rising. This is justified by the increase of complexity.

Collaboration helps to manage complexity and the greater the complexity the more necessary the collaboration. We have to "move closer together". A "lone wolf" is going to be quickly overwhelmed.

The growing dependency goes hand in hand with a higher reciprocal influence; and influence has a strong positive correlation with power. Both – influence and power – are social phenomena.

Within a distinctly social context we cannot increase these social phenomena absolutely. We can only change the ratio – the gain of one side is the loss of the other.

This relative variability needs social responsibility. The use of power and influence without social responsibility damage or destroy a social context. Social responsibility without power and influence is not possible.

---

[1] In the whole text the masculine form is used for persons of both genders.

In a world of growing complexity we will be needing a higher degree of social responsibility, but instead we have realized – and we are going to find – an increasing degree of egoistical individuality. Attack and defense are going to show a strong growth trend, while collaboration is going to shrink.

There are a lot of singles, a lot of people who are lonely in the collective. There are a lot of reservations regarding dissidents, people of other religions, etc. There are a lot of companies which try to survive in a "hypercompetition". There are a lot of people who act according to the motto: "There can only be one!" And all of these continue.

A waxing isolation and egocentrism will be coming to the fore without specific interventions, whereas social responsibility will be taking a back seat. Here, too, there are no signs of change.

A strong manifestation of egocentrism infiltrates social solidarity, and it will be destroying – in the final analysis – our social system.

We have the chance to prevent this destructive process. For this purpose we require social responsibility. In everyday life decision makers certainly go another way. They think that more and more detailed laws, voluntary agreements, etc. ensure a fair and social cooperation. We try to replace social solidarity and responsibility by explicit rules (e.g. laws).

This replacement is not helpful. It is shaping up a tougher conflict between new laws and other rules on one hand as well as more and more egoistical people who try to get around the rules, try to bend the law, etc. In this conflict we will be losing all in the end.

It shows that more and more sophisticated rules cannot substitute social responsibility. We need laws, voluntary agreements, etc., but only in a context of social responsibility.

We need a close interaction between responsibility and solidarity on one hand and explicit "guidelines" on the other hand. In the current process we "suffocate" social responsibility.

Let us realize what we need – today and much more in the future.

Normally the people who damage our social coexistence are not malicious – most people are not aware of this development.

Furthermore, none of us can stop this process within an evolution development. But we can put off the evil hour. We can ensure – today and in the future – that we and the next generations can live appropriately during a longer period of time.

We can ensure that enough of us will be able to act socially responsible on an acceptable scale in a growing complexity and will also be able to remain socially responsible. Each of us is called upon to foster important parts of the foundation for our coexistence – as far as it is possible.

Beyond individual activities we have to implement systematic interventions on a social level, which are able to reach millions of people. Social responsibility has to be a bulk project; individual activities alone are not enough.

A lot of systematic interventions must be implemented in pre-schools and schools. Both must attach great importance to social responsibility. (Pre-)Schools influence a lot of or all people in a society. They are the greatest multipliers. They are responsible to foster the most or all children and adolescents to manage their life, to be able to act appropriately in a complex world, to support the social development.

The support contains the demand to develop the children and the adolescents towards an entrepreneur, because entrepreneurs have all requirements to act socially responsible over the long term.

From my point of view, time is of the essence to deal with social responsibility in a world of increasing complexity. If we fail, our society cannot be survived in a long term.

If we fail, we will be destroying our social structure and our society.

Let´s wake up now. We have no time to lose.

I would particularly like to thank Deon Reinders who proof-read the text which would have never been published without her effort.

Hans-Peter Hummel

Contents

1 Social responsibility as a rising challenge

Social responsibility is becoming increasingly important and more difficult to realize.

Social responsibility means to assume responsibility for our own activities, attitudes, thoughts, etc. and partly the responsibility for other people. The responsibility for ourselves is important to take over responsibility for others.

The responsibility for others appears when our influence on them in a specific sub-area is greater than their influence on us. We have a (determining) influence on what the others plan, what they decide, how they act, etc. We reduce their freedom with our influence, with our power, and we have to assume the responsibility for this influence, for this power[2].

Our responsibility for others has always to do with our power and freedom, and – as a consequence – with our possibilities to reduce the freedom and the power of other people. In every social context an extension of power and freedom on the one hand reduces the power and freedom on the other hand. Power and freedom are only shifted from one system to another – the total quantity remains the same.

Freedom and power interact positively – the greater our freedom, all the more power we can realize and vice versa.

We as powerful people should answer questions such as: Which effects have my decision and my behavior on other actors? Are negative consequences for some people or other systems appropriate in a general view? Can I compensate negative effects during the time? Do I take advantage of some people or target groups?

We take over power and freedom from others and "fill the gap" with responsibility.

---

[2] see, for example, Hummel [2017]

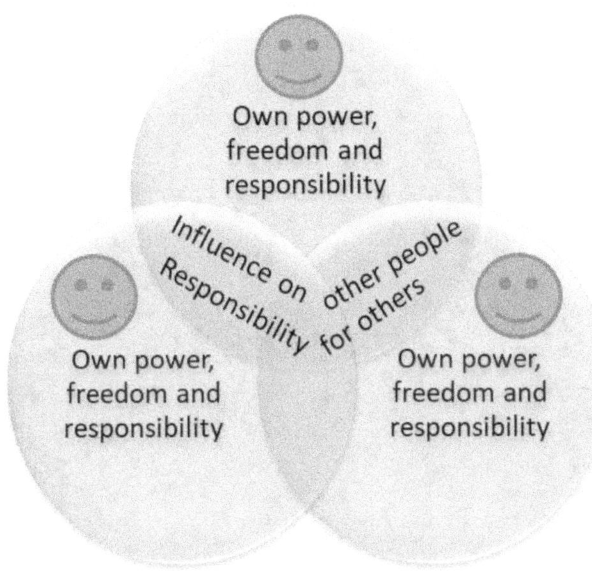

Figure 1: Social responsibility depending on power and freedom (an illustration)

The interplay between power, freedom and responsibility in a social context is only one challenge. Our environment reduces our possibilities to achieve our objectives in a substantially planned direction, because our world is becoming more complex, and with a greater complexity we will be having more problems to achieve our goals by planned activities. In a complex world "a wing beat of a butterfly can cause a severe storm", and we do not know the reasons. We recognize the results. The processes are in a "black box". We will decreasingly understand what is happening around us. The extent of a "black box" will increase, and our power and freedom will decrease the more complexity rises.

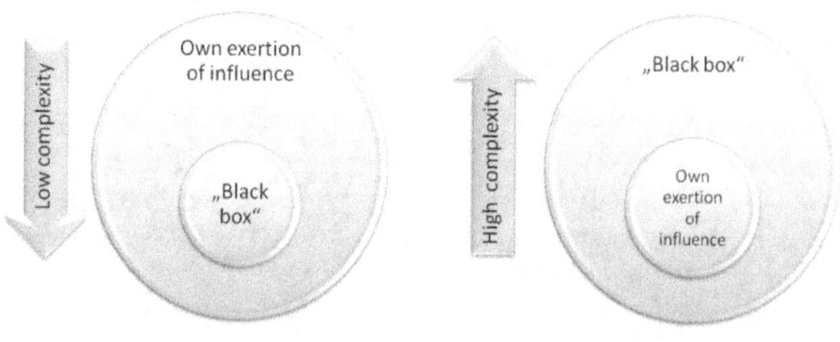

Figure 2: The relationship between complexity, the own exertion of influence and system-specific processes of self-regulation (an illustration)

We will predict the future less and less often and the period of time for a more or less ensured prediction is becoming even shorter. We will be depending on our environment in a waxing extent.

In consequence of this development we are going to assume less and less often the social responsibility for our activities.

We notice that the environment around us get even more confusing and we stand to lose orientation and certainty.

In a confusing world a lot of us tend to retreat and wish for an easier world with a higher stability.

We are susceptible to statements and promises of people who give (supposedly) easy solutions for complex problems. There is a danger that we follow people who give a feeling of security and orientation with simple images and catchwords.

If people with purportedly easy solutions find enough followers to form a group, the members of this group can act socially responsible – but only within their own group, on a level with seemingly reduced complexity. They can realize a strong group cohesiveness; but there is the risk that they exclude all the others. In this process the group members are "the good guys" and all the others are "the bad guys".

As a last consequence, it is possible that they will fight against "the bad guys". All the others irritate the easy thinking, the illusion of an easy solution and a straightforward world. They will try to defend their plain worldview – all the more if the leader pushes it.

Another possibility is that people will backtrack from the overextending world. In this scenario, they become passive and can give up hope as a result of the ever-increasing loss of control wich is accompanied by an ever-increasing fear.

Whatever overextended people do, they reduce their field of action and the greater the complexity increases the more limited their field of action becomes. They reduce their social responsibility and their capability to act appropriately in a social context more and more. They do not contribute to the social responsibility in the (whole) society.

Overextended people have few alternatives and it is important to achieve this level as late as possible. We differ from the level of complexity which we can manage. Some of us lose our "management capabilities" earlier than others.

This knowledge is important even if all of us get caught up in the maelstrom of complexity one day or other; with the consequence that we sooner or later will be reducing our "management capabilities".

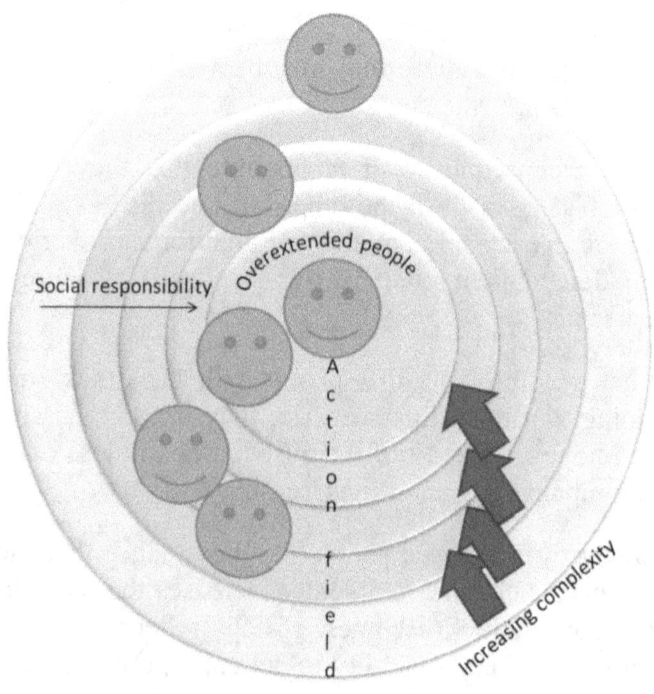

Figure 3: Overextended people reduce their action field in a more and more complex world (an illustration)

The more of us lose our "management capabilities", the fewer of us have to bear the burden of social responsibility.

In order to delay this process we have to support the action ability of people who are at risk of losing it. It is important that humans, so many as possible, maintain their social responsibility and / or should increase it. We must support them to manage their life (a little bit) better and longer. It is increasingly necessary.

We cannot stop the development which increase our problems to manage the environment, but we can – and we should – slow down the process, as far as possible.

If we are socially responsible and if we foster the social responsibility of other people who have problems to manage their life, we generate essential advantages in the active and passive area.

In the active part we help others at once – they obtain capacity building.

In the passive part we can take the pressure off others. If more people are socially responsible, we have a larger basic population and more trusting people. It is not necessary to check everything in this context, because socially responsible people do not "pull others over the barrel". Trusting people reduce the possible alternatives – with their interactions – and the perceived complexity.

The active and passive parts together allow it to develop a stronger foundation for socially responsible activities.

<table>
<tr><td colspan="2" align="center">A higher degree of social responsibility which helps our (whole) society.</td></tr>
<tr><td>Justified trust in people with a higher degree of social responsibility.</td><td>Support from people with a higher degree of ability to act, so that the encouraged others can increase their social responsibility.</td></tr>
</table>

Figure 4: People with a higher degree of social responsibility can help others to act socially responsible (an illustration)

A high degree of social responsibility is a foundation for a still higher degree of social responsibility and accompanied by a less complexity people perceive.

Accompanied by a higher degree of social responsibility the power and freedom increase. In the end we create a helpful, tending upwards spiral. Social responsibility is facilitated, and more people can utilize and extend their social responsibility.

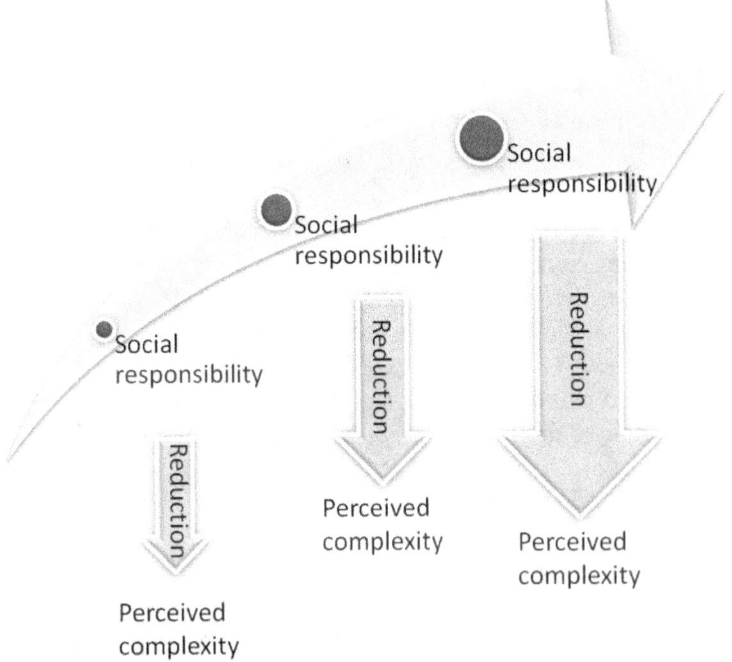

Figure 5: Social responsibility increase social responsibility and reduce the perceived complexity (an illustration)

Furthermore, at a societal level institutions, such as the school system, have to foster an appropriate degree of social responsibility. Social responsibility is an individual as well as a social subject. It is important in every system of a multi-level structure.

Highlights:

- ➢ *Power, freedom and social responsibility go hand in hand.*
- ➢ *We are only responsible if we have freedom to decide, to act, etc.*
- ➢ *If we influence other people attributable to our power, we have to assume the responsibility for the respective topics – we assume social responsibility.*
- ➢ *In a more complex world fewer and fewer of us are able to act socially responsible. We cannot stop this natural process, but we can slow down it.*
- ➢ *We as a more powerful and socially responsible people can help others twofold:*
  - o *as trusting people – wherefore others can reduce the perceived complexity,*
  - o *with our support – whereby others can increase their social responsibility and their management options over a longer period of time.*
- ➢ *People who are overwhelmed*
  - o *are susceptible for feigned easy solutions,*
  - o *backtrack to a smaller playing field,*
  - o *have a tendency*
    - ▪ *to fight against others, who irritate the illusion of an easy solution and a straightforward world, or*
    - ▪ *to give up hope.*
  - o *do not contribute to the social responsibility in the (whole) society.*

2 Requirements for social responsibility in a more difficult context

In a more and more difficult context social responsibility is depended progressively on individuals with specific and outstanding requirements.

It is easy to act socially responsible if all the others around us are socially responsible, too. In this context there are a lot of rules, norms and traditions which help us to act accordingly. We do not need to be personally involved. The environment determines a narrowly defined framework. This framework is independent of us as a one single person. Only a group with a lot of power and assertiveness can change the system during the time. The social system is most important, the individuals accept a subordinate role to the social system.

On the other hand, if nobody is socially responsible, it is very difficult for us to show a social behavior. All the others are against this behavior. They try to suppress the behavior. They impose sanctions on it. They attack us and our social responsibility or they exclude us. The egoistic and egocentric people bring a lot of pressure to bear on us as socially responsible actors.

To be socially responsible in this hostile context, a markedly high degree of individual strength, resilience[3], etc. is necessary. We are personally involved. We have to "fight" against different norms, traditions, etc. We have to assert ourselves against great oppositions, a high intensity of pressure, etc. And we have to resist against egoistical people who have a far lower inhibition threshold to fight against socially responsible people – all the more if they have the norms, traditions and a lot of other people on their side.

In historical times and in the present times there were / are a lot of people who went / go this dangerous way (e.g. Martin Luther King, Mohandas Karamchand Gandhi, Nelson Mandela). A lot of them risk / risked their life to achieve an ambitious social objective.

In a marked-based and socially oriented society both extreme situations are rare. But between the two extreme positions there are a lot of possibilities to act more or less socially responsible – with a different need of personal involvement. And if we accept progressive difficulties to act socially responsible, we need a personal commitment in an ever-increasing degree.

---

[3] see for example Goldstein & Brooks (eds.) [2013], Reich, Zautra & Hall (eds.) [2010] or Glicken [2006]

Caused by the fact that the level of personal commitment must be increased and more and more of us become unable to manage our environment, we will discuss some examples of requirements on the following pages which we need in this more egoistic and egocentric process.

2.1 A deep and wide foundation of information

One important prerequisite for socially responsible activities is the possibility to receive adequate information about the relevant subjects.

Adequate information equally contains wide and profound information. Both are necessary; only one issue is insufficient.

A wide foundation of information contains the possibility to oversee the field. And often, it is essential to look at the subjects from outside, to see the "whole picture", to observe the activities from a "helicopter perspective". So long as we are in a system, we cannot look beyond the horizon.

The following example illustrates this point: On the assumption that people have lived their whole life in a small region with very high walls at the borders. It seems that the walls rise into the sky. Nobody has left the region, nobody have come into the region. Nobody has had contact with people outside their own region. They have had only region-specific experiences. The people do not know what is outside their region. They do not know something about the interaction between their own region and the "things" outside. They have had ideas and imaginations; perhaps there are aliens with five eyes and six arms outside, perhaps it is a fire-spitting hell, a marvelous paradise, dangerous monsters, etc. They can have diverse ideas and imaginations, but they have had no credible information.

Credible information is possible, if they can look beyond the horizon, if they can scale the wall, if they increase their information, if they can dissociate from restrictive attitudes and traditions, from their constricted experiences, perceptions, etc.

In addition, to have a clear view, we need a deep foundation of information in the relevant parts of the field. Only a wide foundation of information is not sufficient.

Without a certain depth, the wide range of information alone has no substance. It is necessary to develop a deeper understanding in the relevant subjects. It is consequential to know what is important in the different parts of the field, what is necessary for the sustainable success, which effects and side-effects are possible, etc.

Without a certain depth we do not know what we do. We "jump on bandwagons", and if the "wind blows stronger", we will "blow away by the wind". We have no foundation, no sustainable strategy. We jump from subject to subject.

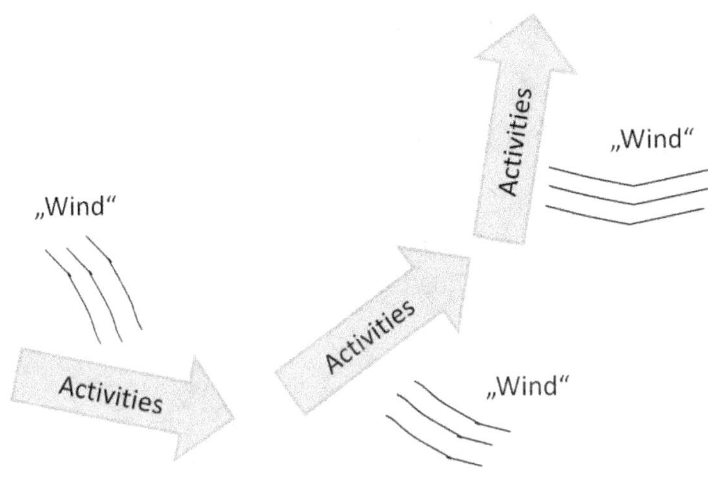

Figure 6: A wide foundation without deepness is not a foundation (an illustration)

On the other hand, if we only have a deep foundation of information, we have less potential for an easy and valid result, because we do not have a general view which makes a "cross-thematic" transfer possible. A deep foundation of information runs into danger of continuing to narrow down our perspective. In this case we "miss the forest for the trees". We "plunge down" into a greater level of detail and do not recognize a larger context.

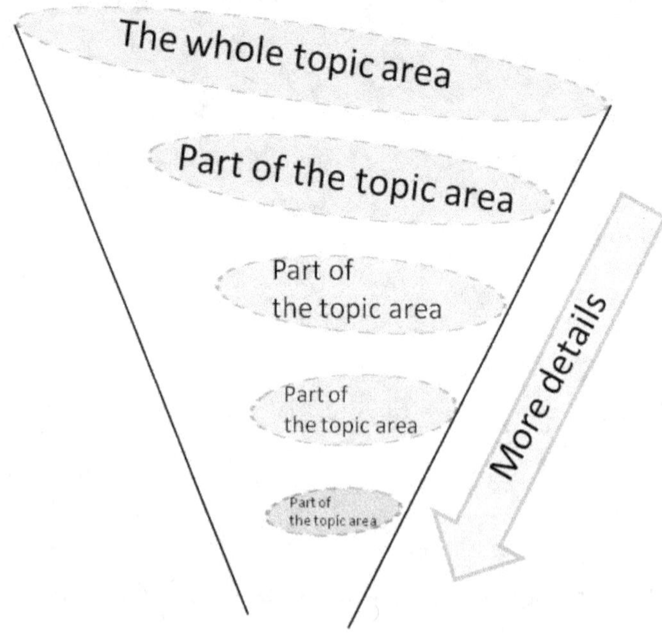

Figure 7: Only a deep foundation of information narrows down the perspective (an illustration)

The critical aspects become visible in different areas. Science is only one example. Scientists tend to narrow down to specific fields if research moves forward. They increase the segmentations and delimitations, and succumb to the temptation all too easily to divide the different fields of action excessively. They risk to reduce or lose the overview.

Simultaneously with a greater segmentation, scientific fields erode in other scientific fields, so that boundaries dissolve. Most often the number of interfaces increase and the borders to other topic areas will be more ill-defined and / or subjective.

The "erosion" follows after the segmentation so that the extension happens in the restriction. Another possibility is that the "erosion" is the beginning of a differentiation. Finally, it is comparable with social responsibility in a world with stronger complexity, where people can act socially responsible within a reduced action field.

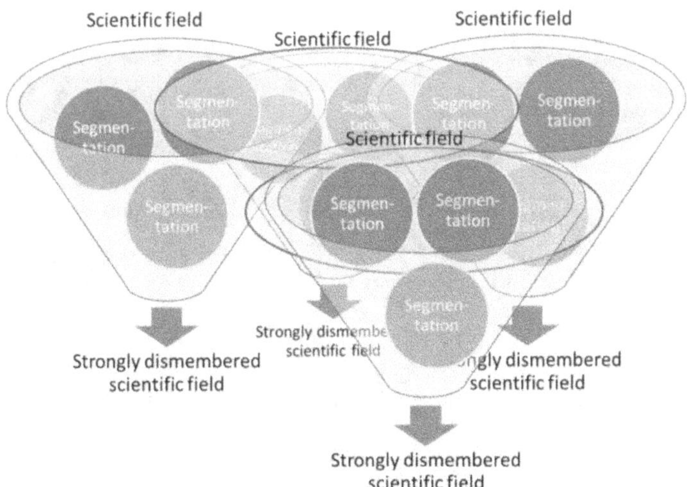

Figure 8: Extension follows the segmentation or is the beginning of segmentation (an illustration)

A deep and wide foundation of information goes beyond these processes and requires a high degree of interactions between the different information fields. It is not enough to connect two subjects and slide into markedly detailed information; a lot of different information and interfaces between many subjects on different levels of segmentation are essential.

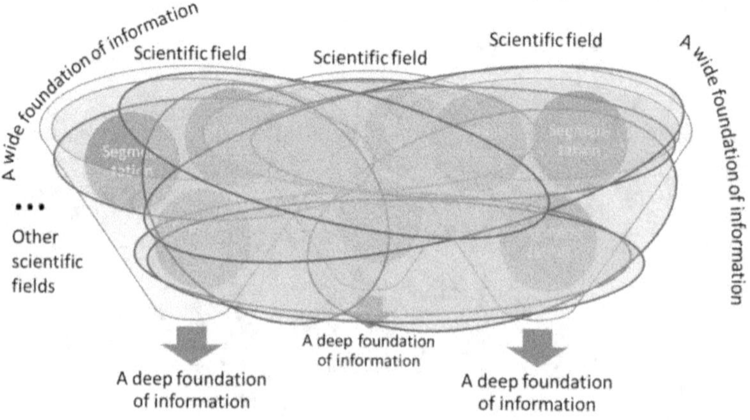

Figure 9: A deep and wide foundation of information needs a high cross-linking level (an illustration)

A high cross-linking level requires marked capabilities to digest the information appropriately. It is necessary that we have procedures and heuristics, for example, which match the different information, which combine them, etc.

Every single information taken by itself is not critical for the sustainable process. It is the combination and the coordination of different information which increase our fitness, our sustainable success. And it is necessary to draw the correct conclusions.

With these capabilities we can look for coherencies and differences, we can weight the different inputs, we are able to decide when it is appropriate to analyze something deeper or to apply a rough estimate, etc. The wide and deep foundation of information is valuable with the assistance of cognitive "governance mechanisms".

These different heuristics, methods, procedures, etc. are unconscious in many cases, with a direct access to our intuition and therefore to an enormous reservoir of problem solving, decision making processes, and other possibilities.

This enormous reservoir gives us the opportunity to develop bigger systems of problem solving, etc. in a process of self-organization, which allow us to handle a higher degree of complexity. We become better and better, do nothing in our conscious part of the mind and gain free space for other cognitive activities. We can go deeper and wider.

The many and varied acquisition of information is an extreme challenge for us, and we need stopping criterions so that we do not overwhelm ourselves. One criterion of the truncation is, if we "juggle too many balls at once", if we have not enough time to busy ourselves with deeper information in the different subjects, if we "jump" from subject to subject, we have to reduce the number of subjects we handle at the same time.

More difficult are the stop criterions for the in-depth information. An easy procedure is not possible because all decisions are situation-dependent. Very roughly we can say: Stop further fine-tuning if the information is not longer accessible to the conscious mind. If we have job relevant and critical information, for example, and we do no longer know that we have this information, because it "becomes the second nature" to us, we are on the way to go into too much detail.

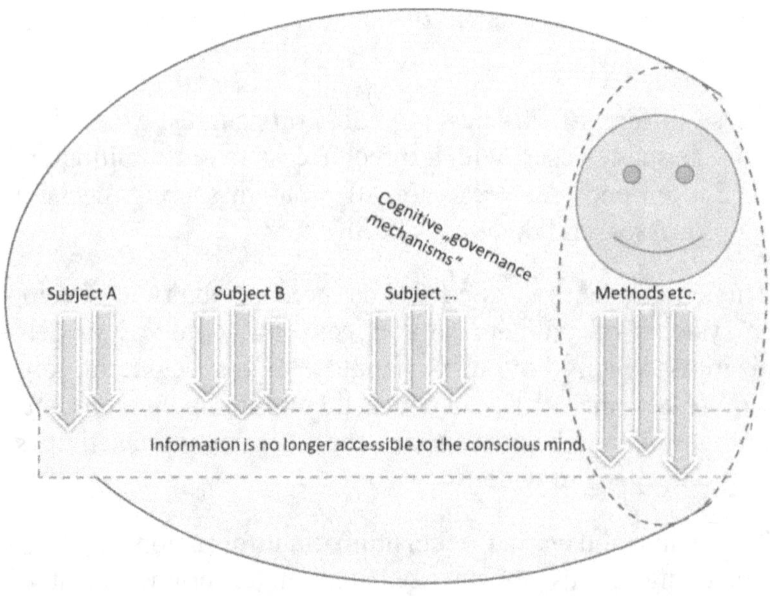

Figure 10: Deep and wide foundation of information with cognitive "governance mechanisms" (an illustration)

To put it simply it is possible to say that

- a deep and wide foundation of information in combination with appropriately cognitive "governance mechanisms" have a high possibility to support easy and valid results,

- a deep foundation of information complicates the cognitive output many a time,

- "subject hopping" without thoughtfulness leads to insubstantial results.

A deep and wide foundation of information in combination with appropriately cognitive "governance mechanisms" is a necessary part of our intuition as a more comprehensive system.

Intuition coordinates and manages all of our perceptions, internal information, conscious and unconscious emotions, etc. and concentrates on the large and complex variety of possibilities into an often easy and valid result.

Intuition is more impactful in a (very) complex situation than an analytical point of view which is too error-prone and too slow.

A deep and wide foundation of information with considerably and appropriately cognitive "governance mechanisms" is necessary in a complex world and part of an overall constellation.

2.2 Intrinsic motivation

In principle we have two pattern of motivation: the intrinsic and the extrinsic motivation. Both can come out more or less strong in every situation.

We have an intrinsic motivation, if something is important for us, if it is an inner urge, if we have fun doing things, etc. Then we develop the motivation on our own terms. We are the "founder" of our motivation.

With an extrinsic motivation we do something because we get advantages from our environment. We approximately get money for our work or a higher status. We are managed. The environment regulates our activities. If a carrot is "dangled" in front of us, we will "run after" it. With a diminishing utility the extrinsic motivation is decreased.

An intrinsic motivation means that we are the master of it.

The extrinsic motivation is depended on the environment which dominates us. We need others who give rewards. We are controlled externally. We are marionettes.

In a progressively complex world with a decreasing social responsibility and an evermore egoistic and egocentric orientation, we are going to have benefits for socially responsible activities at infrequent intervals.

Social responsibility "is going to fall behind" and is going to lose relevance – for people with a high degree of extrinsic motivation.

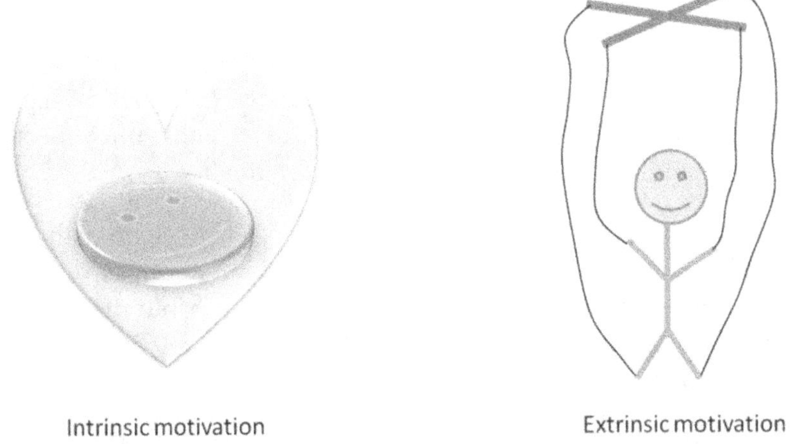

Figure 11: The difference between intrinsic and extrinsic motivation (an illustration)

On the other hand, the relevance of the intrinsic motivation can be retained if we resist the pressure from the outside. Necessary to that end is a great degree of individuality; the possibility to maintain our own values, norms, attitudes, etc. even if others go another way.

2.3 Individuality

The need for our individuality correlates or depends negatively on social responsibility – less social responsibility in our environment requires a high degree of individuality.

Without a high degree of individuality, we "float with the current" – more or less –, we do what people in our environment do, we are a part of the mainstream. We disappear into the crowd. We are managed by the multitude with a low degree of freedom. We are hangers-on.

Only if we have a high individual alignment, we are able to "swim against the tide". We can maintain our own (core) values, our own norms, attitudes, etc. We decide for ourselves. We have the freedom to plan, to decide, to act, etc. We can realize a high degree of responsibility even if all the others around us disapprove.

Individuality by itself can be utilized in a context of social responsibility or in a framework of egoism respectively egocentricity. Accordingly, it is necessary to clarify that individuality is an expedient to realize socially responsible behavior. Individuality without social responsibility is antisocial. Social responsibility without individuality cannot survive social pressure.

Furthermore, individuality does not mean that we are loners. We know that we cannot change our environment alone, that we cannot strengthen the social responsibility in the society alone. We are team players too, but we "set the agenda" – the social "agenda".

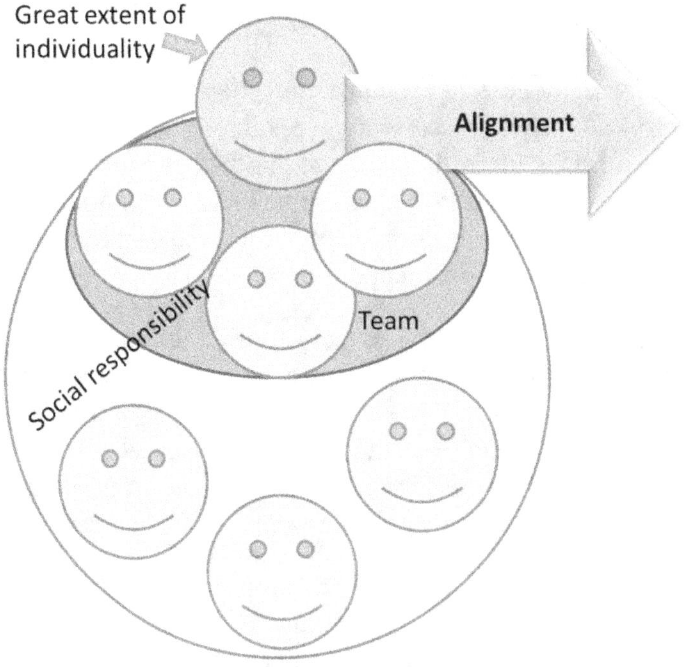

Figure 12: The necessity of individuality and social responsibility

As far as we live in a more egoistic and egocentric environment we need a lot of different traits of character, personality traits, attitudes, etc. to act socially responsible. Some of them are:

- self-confidence and a perceived self-efficacy,

- resilience,

- self-determination.

Self-confidence and a perceived self-efficacy

If a lot of people act against our social priorities, it is important to know that we can achieve something, no matter what the others do. It is important to have "both feet planted firmly on the ground" also in the face of pushback. It is important that we have an internal evaluation system which has a higher priority than the external social influence.

If we have a high level of self-confidence and a perceived self-efficacy, we will have trust in a process; even without the comprehensive control. We know that what we do work somehow or other. We know that there isn`t just one way of doing it. Nobody can restrain us from achieving the objective, from achieving a high degree of social responsibility.

If we have a high level of self-confidence and a perceived self-efficacy, we have no fear of failure. And we have no existential fear. We know that failures are part of the life and we have the trust that the next success is coming after a failure. We trust the process of life, because we trust ourselves. We do not doubt, we trust "down to the last fiber", with our heart and mind. Doubts are not a part of our mind.

We do not spare a thought about a long-term defeat. We know – deep within our heart – that we will be successful over time, no matter how difficult the path is.

Every mistake, every failure is only a learning opportunity which helps us to become successful.

Resilience

If we are under pressure and negatively evaluated stress (hereinafter referred to as stress) it is difficult to behave fitly, because situations are very encumbering and burdens hamper the opportunities for actions. We should strive to act calmly, circumspectly, etc.

Normally stress is not a good advisor in a complex situation. Stress can raise our fear and can reduce the possibility to think straight if the stress is strong enough.

Figure 13: Resilience foster, burdens hamper the opportunities for action (an illustration)

If stress is not strong enough to reduce our ability to act currently, we can get problems in the future anyway, because stress accumulates. Stress does not reduce completely if the stress situation is over – even less if stress is repeated at frequent intervals. We store stress and in the next stressful situation we are therefore under stress earlier.

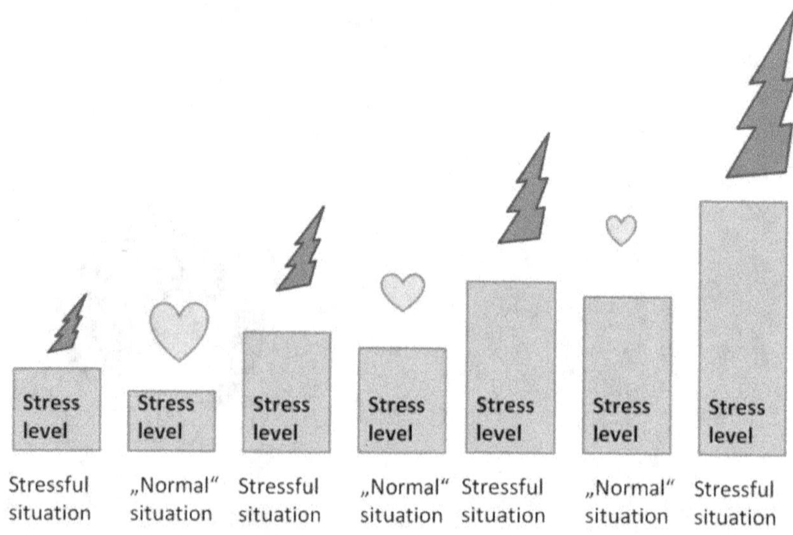

Figure 14: Stress is accumulated over more stressful situations in a process (an illustration)

Stress leads to a very powerful problem: If it is accumulated, we get problems in ever easier situations. Burnout is a very good example for this process.

At the same time, we will be going through a higher and higher degree of complexity, where stress proves to be a "disastrous advisor".

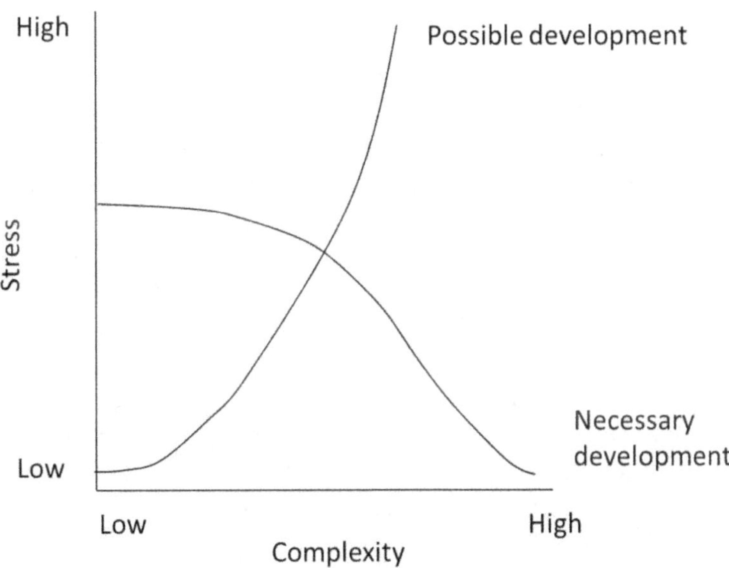

Figure 15: The necessary and possible development between complexity and stress (an illustration)

Stress damages – with a substantial speed – what we need in a growing extent and reduce our ability to act.

We are going to get into trouble because our environment is going to continuously determine our life and this is going to turn us into a puppet.

Stress is one of the greatest "groundbreaker" which is destroying society.

When we accelerate in a downward spiral, we can realize an upward spiral just as well; a spiral helps us to act appropriately in evermore encumbering situations. It is not natural to be hectic and "stressed out". It is possible to have a high degree of resilience.

Resilience has psychological as well as physiological and social reasons. It interacts with transmitter releases, hormones and the hormonal changes, trace elements, organs and their correct functions, etc. It interacts with cognitive, emotional and conative aspects as well as the perception and the behavior with the environmental responses which depend on social norms, traditions, statutory requirements, etc.

Resilience and stress are influenced by complex interactions, with a general view of all physiological and psychological aspects in a social context. Psychological, physiological and social aspects work together in a complex way and influence the perception of stress.

The perception of stress and the resilience involve the holistic person, and the best bet is to be resilient on a sufficient level.

If we should optimize the level, we can become successful very quickly or very slowly. It can be very easy because an intervention at one point changes the whole system in order that one intervention can lead to a magnificent success.

It can be very difficult because every intervention can lead to a tremendous problem. The interactions between all the different things are very complex with a high degree of self-organization. We do not know what can happen if we change one aspect. The result of changing one point can vary between "catastrophic results" up to "objectives are fully met".

If we do not depend on one intervention, we can stimulate the system at various points – and hope that the different stimuli operate in the desired direction.

We cannot control the whole system but we can gain experiences, and if we reflect on the different experiences, we can get a better feel for different effects.

A better feel for different effects assumes an intense preoccupation with these topics. It is important to get a feel for the different interventions and for the cooperation to increase the resilience. It is necessary to evolve a deep and wide foundation of information.

We may assume that only a few of us can bring oneself to build enough information as necessary. This way is effortful. A lot of us want to have it easier the more challenges we have. They back off from the effort.

If we do not want to invest in this development, we have two other possibilities:

- to live with rising problems,

- to consult an expert.

The first alternative is not helpful whereas the possibility to utilize an external control for our own development can be an appropriate way. It can help us to save our own resources and to reduce the number of mistakes.

No matter if we prioritize the self-controlling or the external control, it is important for us to increase our resilience because we have to be able to stay on top of things, to stay calm, circumspect, etc. And perhaps we like the challenges and we are "juggling" with the different possibilities.

Self-determination

As long as we have a great self-determination, we take care of our own values, our own ethical reference system. It is not important for us to be everybody's friend. It is not necessary for us to be part of the mainstream.

We act proactive; intrinsically motivated and with a high degree of self-controlling.

We as self-determined people accept the individuality and – in a social context – the responsibility for other people. We act socially responsible independent of others around us and their behavior patterns.

Highlights:

- ➢ *With decreasing popularity of social responsibility the personal involvement is on the rise.*
- ➢ *If we give social responsibility an important value in an environment which disprizes it, we will need – for example – a*
  - o *deep and wide foundation of information — with appropriately cognitive "control mechanisms",*
  - o *distinctly intrinsic motivation,*
  - o *strong individuality which gives us the possibility to go our own social but independent way.*
- ➢ *The cognitive "governance mechanisms" can work unconsciously, so that we gain free space for other cognitive activities.*
- ➢ *A deep foundation of information should end before the information is no longer accessible to the conscious mind.*
- ➢ *A distinctly intrinsic motivation helps social responsibility – an extrinsic motivation damages it if we need a highly and progressively personal involvement.*
- ➢ *A strong individuality with a social orientation needs, for example,*
  - o *a high level of self-confidence,*
  - o *perceived self-efficacy,*
  - o *marked resilience and the same*
  - o *self-determination.*

3 An entrepreneur is socially responsible

An entrepreneur can act socially responsible under very difficult conditions.

From my point of view, an entrepreneur has the requirements for social responsibility in a high manifestation. He is predestinated to realize a high degree of social responsibility.

An entrepreneur shapes markets or other systems on a comparable level of complexity [Hummel, 2015]. In these very complex systems he creates outstanding things; leaves very strong and often irreversible footprints.

To create companies is not enough for an entrepreneur. A company is a means to an end. It is a vehicle to shape markets or other systems on a comparable level of complexity.

An entrepreneur thinks big and acts appropriately in very complex situations. It is not necessary for an entrepreneur to develop new things. He can utilize the same products, processes, etc. as other market players, but he marks themselves off from others to a great extent. An entrepreneur stands out at a great distance from the other actors.

An entrepreneur goes his own way. He does not accept the mediocrity. He does not accept the lowest common denominator. An entrepreneur is unafraid of failures and with his consistent activities he evolves a lot of power and a great assertiveness.

He knows he will achieve his targets, and along the way he is flexible. He accepts that he cannot manage everything.

We come face to face with "coincidences" or "(great) misfortunes" – or, in other words, with environment-specific processes of self-organization – and an entrepreneur utilizes the "coincidences" and the "(great) misfortunes" to achieve outstanding targets.

He loves new challenges – the greater the better. And he has an intrinsic motivation to manage these challenges.

To love new challenges implicates a high level of curiosity, multi-layered interests which are based on and come to a wide and deep foundation of information.

He accepts to "reap" discardment and pushback. Other people are against his dream, his targets, and his activities.

What an entrepreneur strives is often unrealistic for other people. They call him an "oddball". They apply pressure and it might be that they exclude the entrepreneur.

An entrepreneur can handle this social pressure, can manage the criticism. He knows that "unrealistic" is a term for here and now. For the future it is of no importance at all. The term "unrealistic" is meant to underline that something does not exist now and people have no idea today, how they can realize it in the future.

We cannot augur the future. We cannot say what is realistic and unrealistic in the coming periods. Anything what humans have developed was unrealistic in the past. The internet was unrealistic at the beginning of the 20th century. The moon landing was unrealistic in the 19th century. And a plane and generally the aviation, as we know it today, were unrealistic in the 18th century.

It is not just that an entrepreneur has to overcome opposition, it is difficult for him to profit by other experiences, because his way is different. He cannot make use of a "beaten path", he has to clear his own way.

To go a new way requires the firm belief that his own activities work. This belief is deeply rooted in his mind.

The foundation is in man himself. It is the confidence the person has in his own activities. It is the trust in a working process; even without the comprehensive control.

An entrepreneur trusts his abilities to find the right way in every situation. He trusts his intuition and his capability to recognize the chance if it is presented to him.

These capabilities are important for a high degree of resilience which is important to manage extraordinary challenges in a (very) complex environment.

An entrepreneur needs a high degree of resilience, it is absolutely essential for his success, partly because he pushes the complexity by his actions. Resilience is a "must-have". It is necessary to act calmly, circumspectly, etc. Hecticness as well as hasty and unsubstantiated activities are contraindicated and hamper the success.

The concept of an entrepreneur contains a high degree of resilience during a long term whereas a lot of other people increase their stress in a more and more complex world.

With his outstanding activities an entrepreneur influences a lot of people – their behaviors, their attitudes, their life –, and he knows that he has to work together with them, that he needs others, that he needs their trust and their commitment. He knows that each and every one of us is dependent on social relationships. The entrepeneur as well as all of us.

An entrepreneur is an individualist and simultaneously social. He has a deep and wide ethical foundation.

He knows that great power requires great social responsibility.

An entrepreneur, with a high degree of social responsibility, can motivate people to work together with him to achieve the objectives the entrepreneur has. He is also team-oriented and independent of others.

To be both team-oriented and simultaneously independent of the social influence and pressure, an entrepreneur has to go the narrow path between "abnormal" – outside the standard – and "normal" – part of the majority. It is necessary that he moves in a proven acceptable range, that he finds common ground with other people; with their attitudes, their norms, etc.

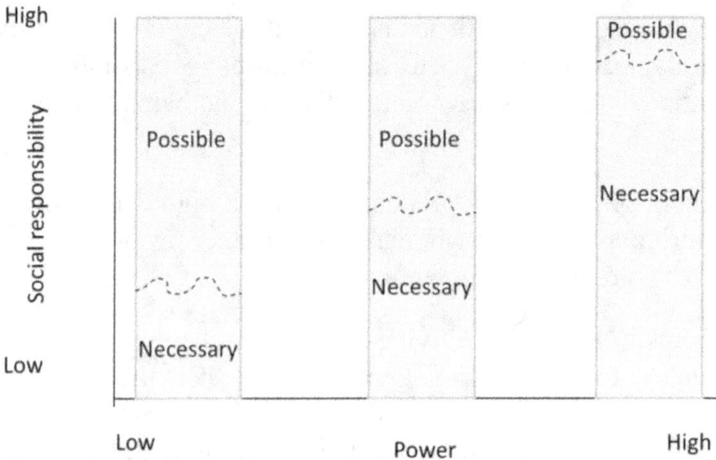

Figure 16: Comparison between power potential and social responsibility (an illustration)

Is there is no common ground, people will not have a foundation for a relationship; they do not have a mutual understanding. They live in "different worlds" and have nothing to do with each other.

An entrepreneur has to be outside and inside the group; certainly he should be more outside than inside.

The interaction or even the collaboration with an entrepreneur is a challenge for other people. The entrepreneur "creates" difficult decisions in a complex environment and his implementations are bristle with obstacles so that he has a lot of chances for heavy defeats. People who work together with him have to accept the volatility and have to trust him – in good times as in bad.

Trust is necessary for people who work together with an entrepreneur, and it is necessary for an entrepreneur himself. It is essential for his survival. Without the trust of the employees, the cooperation partners and other stakeholders, he has very limited opportunities to become successful over a long term.

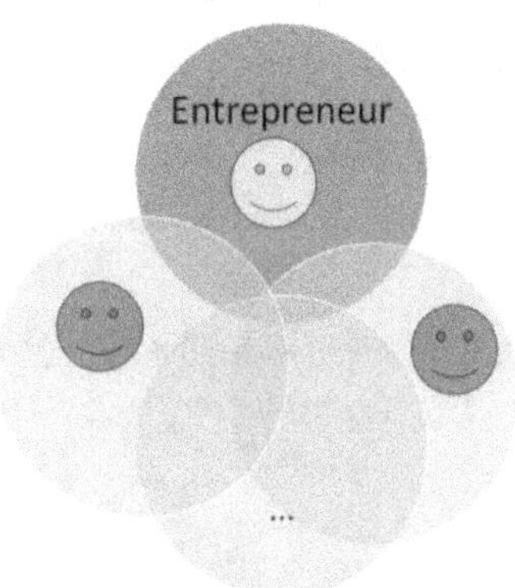

Figure 17: An entrepreneur has to be outside and inside a group (an illustration)

Trust has to remain in force during and after defeats which require a socially responsible behavior on the side of the entrepreneur. Only if the entrepreneur is socially responsible, the stakeholders have to feel certain that the entrepreneur is fair and that he considers their needs appropriately.

For an entrepreneur socially responsible behaviors are nothing out of the ordinary, because he has a deep and wide ethical foundation and social responsibility is an important part of this base.

In summary we can say: an entrepreneur has an exceptionally extensive intersection with people who realize a sufficient degree of social responsibility in the challenging society. And it becomes clear that an entrepreneur is going to be increasingly important if the world around becomes more and more complex. Evermore, other people are going to reach their limits and the number of entrepreneurs is going to be greater in relation to the basic population of socially responsible people.

An entrepreneur is gaining in importance greatly in our economical and social development.

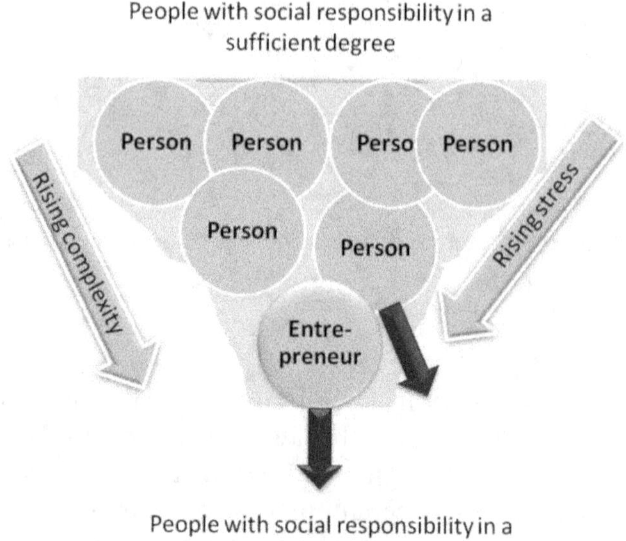

Figure 18: Entrepreneurs are going to be more and more important in increasingly complex situations (an illustration)

Highlights:

- *An entrepreneur is equally individualist and social.*
- *He is predestinated to act socially responsible.*
- *An entrepreneur with a high degree of social responsibility is going to be increasingly important in a world with rising complexity because other people are going to evermore reach their limit.*

4 Social responsibility towards the stakeholders

Stakeholder management needs direct and indirect activities. Direct activities are referred to the sustainable business success. Indirect activities are referred to the sustainable success of the stakeholders in the society.

Social responsibility cannot be comprehensive. We cannot realize it generally in a society. We have to concentrate our socially responsible activities on relevant target groups. In the course of this we should make sure that the border is not too restrictive.

In the private sector this demand can be a problem. In a business context it is easier to recognize the target groups. These are people and groups who are important for the business – in other words, we have to concentrate on the stakeholders.

Stakeholders influence us as business people as well as the company and vice versa. We as business people interact with the customers, the employees, the cooperation partners, the shareholders, perhaps with environmental organizations, etc.

The influence of the stakeholders is, among other things, distinguished from the distribution of power.

When the distribution of power is centralized in a stakeholder community, the power is generally high enough to put pressure on the business partner – and enough power steers the behavior of the partner.

When the distribution of power is decentralized in a stakeholder community, the exercise of power requires the coordination inside the stakeholder group, what may be very difficult. One consequence of this situation is that the others assume that the stakeholder – with a decentralized distribution of power – has no power and can be overlooked or suppressed. There are many examples of this attitude; be it the rotten meat scandals or products with toxic substances, with inferior components, etc.

With the assistance of modern information technologies it is easier to concentrate on the decentralized distribution of power and the fundamental power of the stakeholder in the collectivity is more obvious. A more massive "shitstorm" of angry customers on the internet is only one example. Companies recognize more easily that the customers have power, too. That can help to meet each other "on an equal footing".

We as socially responsible actors do not need the pressure to act "on an equal footing" with the stakeholders, we act fair – no (dirty) tricks, no "talking out of both sides of one´s mouth", no contracts with a "false bottom". We as socially responsible actors know that every stakeholder and every part of the stakeholders are important, deserve acceptance and a fair treatment.

An equated stakeholder management is not easy to realize in a progressively egoistic and egocentric development, because the needs and targets of the different stakeholders are possibly diverse or conflicting. Customers want – for example – cheap products with a high-quality, shareholders want a high dividend, employees want a high remuneration. To achieve everything up to a maximum is not possible, but we can solve the conflict, if we balance the different needs, and if we accomplish an understanding among the stakeholders that this way is the best way for them – not the maximum for one person or group is the best, but rather an appropriate result for every group during the time. A maximum supports a short-term success; balanced success supports a long-term performance.

If we try to balance different activities, we are faced with (great) challenges, and in a continually complex environment more and more people are going to reach their limits. They are going to run the risk to focus on some or only one stakeholder (e.g. the shareholder).

In this focused situation they ignore they variety and hope that the reality follows this course of action. But it does not work, and the most of them know that it does not work, but they have no better alternative – they reach their limits.

Entrepreneurs and other people with comparable competences can deal with the different needs and targets in an ongoing complex environment. They can act fair. They can act socially responsible towards all stakeholders. They can integrate economical, ecological and social components into the business model.

Even if the integration of the three components into the business model is more difficult at the beginning, over a long-term it is more successful, because we have a better chance to create new – and sustainable – products, processes, structures, etc.

A broadly positioned and authentic stakeholder management is also important for trust – all the more in failing phases. Trust is not only important for an entrepreneur, it is important for every business person and company in a world with growing complexity. The stakeholders determine whether a company survives – in good times as in bad. The stakeholders foster the success of the company or they take care of the failure. Trust is necessary to live through a failure. Trust helps that the stakeholders do not turn away; it helps that they remain faithful to the company and the business people in challenging times.

If the stakeholders trust the company and us as the decision makers, they assume that they can count on us. They are sure that we try to change a defeat into a success – for ourselves and all the stakeholders.

If we are able to deal with the different needs and targets and if we seriously try to change defeats into success for ourselves and all stakeholders, we realize an important part of Corporate Social Responsibility (CSR) and – most likely – a sustainable success.

Up to now we have discussed direct activities. A CSR goes beyond the scope of these direct activities and it considers indirect activities which ensure the sustainable success.

Indirect activities are activities without a direct link to the business success. One example is an entrepreneur who acts as a patron [Hummel, 2016]. He supports, for example, the school education, so that the pupils are better equipped to deal with high complexity. The entrepreneur can help young people to manage their lives better in the long-term future with higher complexity. A patron does not rig pupils with subliminal subjects in specifically developed school books, etc. He does not "play a double game". He does not act to achieve an (immediately) direct economically benefit, he tries to ensure the sustainable fitness of the young people and the society over a long period of time.

With indirect activities we exceed the direct business success and foster a sustainably social success. We help the society in a greater extent.

We must realize that the fitness of society is an important requirement for our own sustainable success and for the sustainable success of every stakeholder. Companies, for example, need high qualified employees and cooperation partners on an ongoing basis who can handle the different challenges. They need customers who are able to act consistently in their complex environment. They need a society with citizens who are able to act in a context with increasing complexity, etc.

Each and every one of us is responsible for the sustainable success of society. We are responsible that the subsequent generations can live in a successful society and that they are able to develop it further.

If too many people are unable to cope with the challenges in their life, the social conflicts grow rapidly, the social coexistence is increasingly unstable, the complexity and the dynamic rise disproportionately, and the possibility to realize business success becomes something of a lottery.

Highlights:

> *Social responsibility is aligned to relevant target groups.*
> *Important target groups in a business context are the stakeholders.*
> *Business people should treat all stakeholders suitably, independent of their perceived power.*
> *In a stakeholder management it is important to balance diverse or conflicting targets of the different stakeholders. It is difficult but necessary.*
> *An integration of the economical, ecological and social components can be more difficult at the beginning, but it is helpful during a long-term.*
> *A fair stakeholder management supports the trust, which will be more and more essential for survival.*
> *A stakeholder oriented CSR considers direct and indirect socially responsible activities.*
> *Direct activities in a CSR context refer to a short-term as well as to a long-term business success.*
> *Indirect activities in a CSR context refer to a long-term success for the society and as a result of this to the success for the (partially) integrated systems (e.g. the company).*
> *A social success is necessary for the business success.*

5 Strengthen social responsibility

The requirements for social responsibility liable to conscious and unconscious developments.

Every single one is addressed as well as social institutions.

A great extent of individuality, a deep and wide foundation of information in combination with appropriately cognitive "governance mechanisms" and a high degree of intrinsic motivation require development processes which are started in the early childhood and ended with the death of the person.

Development processes in these contexts base on multiple procedures are influenced by

- individual and unconscious developments,

- context-specific and non-transparent developments,

- individual and conscious processes,

- conscious and planned processes which are managed by others.

5.1 Individual and unconscious developments

Every day we do a lot of different things which are not conscious. We go for a walk without thinking about every step.

Our muscles and our organs work without the conscious exertion of influence.

Black thoughts, sanitary views, helpful ideas, etc. appear in our mind, wax and wane or manifest themselves, and often we do not know where they come from. They are "automatical" in our mind, without conscious activities.

Every day a vast number of activities happen within us and are governed in self-regulated processes without our conscious help. It can be assumed that "… (our) conscious capacity to process information is much less than our unconscious capacity" [Blair, 2010: 51].

The unconsciously most diverse activities influence us permanently – day and night. The nervous system, for example, "… (regulates. Remark of the author) internal bodily functions and provides a means for an organism to adapt to the external environment. In order for an organism to regulate interactions with the external environment and maintain a stable internal milieu, information must flow to and from the brain and spinal cord" [Winters, McCabe, Green & Schneiderman, 2000: 4].

The unconsciously most diverse activities influence a lot of different individual aspects; (conscious) emotions, the perceptions, the behaviors, etc.

We perceive with our sensory system and what plus how it is processed in our brain and in our mind depend on a vast number of unconscious activities and the self-regulated processes.

Some scientists have evidence that conscious decisions and behavior are prepared by the unconsciously cerebral activities in the forefront [Walde, 2006: 48]. Similar comments are made by Rüegg [2011: 162 – 163].

"In fact, much of people´s behavior seems to be based on unconscious … control …" [Blair, 2010: 50].

There are results that unconscious decision processes can improve difficult decisions [Balcetis & Granot, 2015: 342], and it is possible that unconscious, automated processes are necessary for these decisions. "Without the ability to use this type of processing (unconscious processes. Remark of the author), individuals would be bogged down trying to make even the simplest decision" [Blair, 2010: 52]. One possible reason for the relevance is that "… (the) unconscious brain works efficiently because it uses a network of interconnected systems in parallel" [Blair, 2010: 57].

Furthermore, pheromones influence our behavior unconsciously. In one study males at the age of 26 to 42 received every day a pheromone preparation. A reference group received a placebo. Eight weeks later the test group showed an enhanced socio-sexual behavior as the reference group [Reisyan, 2013: 180].

Another cognition is that our "… dopamine system is positioned to alter the propensity to focus conscious attention on a current task versus flexibly altering behavior to more effectively achieve goals" [Grace, 2010: 39].

The unconsciously most diverse activities influence also our attitudes, character traits, our temperament, etc. The authors Rothbart & Bates [2006], for example, give an overview about the influence of unconscious activities on the temperament.

In addition, neuromodulators influence the conscious elements. Ashton, for example, wrote something about an endocannabinoid system which can be "… (possibly) the most powerful and ancient of the modulatory systems that influence every conscious thought and feeling …" [2010: 54].

The examples which show the relevance of unconscious and the influence on conscious activities can be almost extended at will. It shows that our internally self-regulated processes – which are not conscious – are a very important part of our development. All things which dawn on us have interactions with unconscious activities and with our internally self-regulated processes.

Beyond that we recognize that all our social activities – and hence all socially responsible activities, too – are affected by our conscious and – just as important – our unconscious activities.

On the other hand conscious activities influence our unconscious aspects which can change if we develop ourselves. However, the influence is often unspecific.

We cannot manage most of the unconscious activities. We can only influence these parts of our life. In contrast to this our unconscious activities can manage our conscious activities significantly.

In other words, the unconscious activities are the "helmsman" and the "captain" together. Our conscious activities are undertaken "sailors" tasks.

5.2 Context-specific and non-transparent developments

If we work together with a lot of other people, we deal with different interests, with different and possibly changing coalitions, with people who "deal in an underhanded manner" or "put all the cards on the table", etc. If we interact with three or four others, it might be that we can predict the process. In interaction processes with hundreds or thousands of people, we get unexpected results. We have to accept developments outside our control capabilities.

These unexpected results show that we have mechanisms of self-regulation in these interaction systems which are often opaque. We do not know the mechanisms, the effects, the consequences, etc. We recognize results, but what happened before-hand remains widely an open question.

The answers fail to materialize with increasing frequency the more complex a system become. In very complex contexts system specific self-regulated mechanisms drift to and fro like a plaything in the ocean. We cannot manage (very) complex systems, we are managed.

Even if we have little or no management possibilities, we have to realize that systems work. The mechanisms of self-regulation in combination with our activities can work. We can be successful although we cannot manage everything.

Principally, we can establish parallels between this social development and our own conscious and unconscious activities. In either case, we have a combination of separate processes which works without our input, on one hand, and processes we can manage on the other hand. Both parts have an intensive inter-action and every success and failure is influenced by both com-ponents.

We as human beings are the only "system" which is able to act in a bigger and more complex system today. We are necessary for the cultural development. Simultaneously we have "to hand over control". We have to accept the system specific self-regulation. We "want to remain at the wheel, we try to retain what "get out of hand", but we have no chance. Our activities in an evolutionary development support a higher complexity and reduce our management possibilities.

More often we go through "random" or "fateful" results, but in actual fact we deal with system specific self-regulated mecha-nisms in complex systems. Coincidence or destiny are specific mechanisms of self-regulation. They are risen in a more complex world and they exceed our management capabilities at a great pace in this process.

Normally we refuse to believe this development. We try to retain the lead by setting rules which should regulate the (partially) integrated systems. We tighten the laws, expand the voluntary agreements, strengthen the surveillances, etc.

The restrictive rules are increased with a growing complexity and power of the bigger systems.

We try to get back more governance, but we restrict the possibilities, we restrict the necessary flexibility in a continually dynamic world. We try to extend the fitness but we reduce it.

The systems at a higher level strongly "patronize" us. Companies in a financial market are good examples. The "Solvency" and "Basel" regulations should stabilize the branch of industry, but instead they take more and more "the air to breath".

More restrictive rules and surveillances will gain further steam if we go in a more egoistic and egocentric direction, because companies and other systems will be exploiting their freedom – and will be destabilizing the whole social system. The banking market depicts an example, as we have seen in the financial crisis, started in 2007, and with one peak in 2008 – at the time when the bank Lehman Brothers went bankrupt.

It should be added that companies and other systems run the risk to break the laws and other rules if the restrictive rules increase. It becomes lot easier for all systems to cause infringements if almost everything is forbidden.

And if we have more infringements, we tighten the laws and other rules as well as the surveillances.

We run with a considerable speed in a vicious circle and think it helps us to manage our environment. Quite the opposite happens, we ratchet up the problems.

We invest evermore resources (e.g. for the surveillance) which bring about ruin, and we assume that the "abyss" is risen to a "bridge". But an "abyss" cannot become a "bridge".

The attempt to govern everything as gapless as possible also leads to the fact that we reduce and / or hamper the trust of the stakeholders – which is necessary for the company´s survive.

The attempt to retain the governance desperately increases the complexity, reduces the governance, the trust, and our freedom – more than necessary.

Without freedom we are not responsible. A very close-knit or even a "gapless" network of laws and rules abolish – as a last consequence – our freedom and our social responsibility.

We can stop this spiral, we can defer the way in the "gaping abyss" when we increase the social responsibility, the justified trust, etc. All of these are necessary for a life in freedom and for a long-term survival.

Let´s burst the vicious cycle with social responsibility so that we can superiorly trust each other.

On this basis, we can accept the mechanism of self-regulation better in our environment. We can juggle with these comprehensive mechanisms in a greater possibility space.

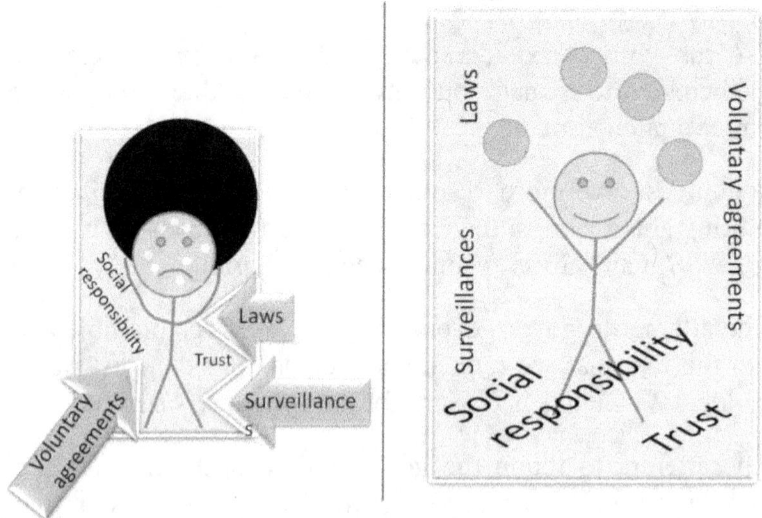

Figure 19: Appropriate and obstructive social rules and surveillances (an illustration)

We need laws, voluntary agreements, surveillances, etc. – they are very important. Nevertheless we have to find a dynamic balance between governance and self-regulation. A greater trust in the mechanisms of self-regulation and a higher social responsibility help to recognize the right extent of governance, and prevents overshooting.

5.3 Individual and conscious processes

Considering the unconscious processes, we have scope to decide what we want to do. We can decide to act more egoistic or social. We are not other-directed exclusively, we are self-determined, too. In a challenging world, we can decide to learn as much as possible. We can set objectives. We can look for practices to achieve the objectives. We can decide to go another way if the current way is unrewarding.

For all these decisions we need knowledge as an essential foundation. In this day and age we have a lot of different possibilities to improve our knowledge – more than in the previous era.

We live in a time of information overload and have to implement strategies to utilize the many and varied information for our development. Information is not a scarce resource; quite the contrary, it becomes more and more a burden.

The "world wide web" is not only important for knowledge, it is also important for our communication. We can "tap" the internet to communicate with people around the world and share our experience with them. We can learn from people who live in different cultures. And we can learn from our neighbors. We have a "window to the world" and a "door" to our neighbors.

Knowledge and experience have no borders. We can principally say that we live in an open society without unscalable hierarchies.

We can plan our life and our development as no other generation before.

To utilize the different helpful possibilities, curiosity and the interest in different things are important aspects. The most of us are generally curious and interested in different things at an early age. "A child's curiosity is innate and undeniable … Curiosity compels us to connect with the world …" [Benson & Di Biase, 2015: 21]. As children and perhaps as teenagers as well as young adults we have fun to learn, we like to make experiences, we love to discover the world [Benson & Di Biase, 2015]. We expand our experiences, and we can combine our unconscious and our conscious parts. We challenge our freedom and try to extend it.

In adulthood there are a lot of us who do not see the advantages of curiosity. Taberner & Taberner Siggins wrote some years ago, for example, that curiosity is an innate gift, "… but as adults this natural gift is forgotten or dampened down for a variety of reasons" [2015: xi].

When we lose our curiosity, our interest in new discoveries, etc. we run into danger to reduce our fitness, our ability to manage the challenges in our life.

It is important that we are curious and interested in new discoveries at any age. It is important to make mistakes, to learn from our mistakes, to reflect on our experiences, our current situation and a possible future.

Curiosity and an interest in new discoveries are cornerstones for a deep and wide foundation of information. And together with the reflection about the different experiences, the current situation and the possibilities in the future, we have important components to develop appropriately cognitive "governance mechanisms".

In a more and more complex world it is difficult to sustain or to extend the curiosity, an interest in new discoveries, etc. The changes will be too fast, the disorientation will be too intense. The self-determination subsides more and at a quicker rate.

One important aspect to ensure our self-determination is to be resilient. Too many possibilities increase the stress – or at least the potential of stress. Therefore it is important to reduce this potential so that resilience has a chance.

With a high degree of resilience we can integrate our curiosity, our interest in new discoveries, etc. in a positive action ability.

Resilient people are longer able to act. They have diverse sense of achievements and pleasure in new challenges. New things are not a danger for them, new things are exciting.

The question how we can improve our resilience is difficult to answer because there are a lot of interacting possibilities.

On a global level the relaxation has an important status. "The more we are relaxed, then the less we are stressed" [Shields, 2012: 115], and the better is the ability to act appropriately in an encumbering situation. Relaxation helps us to be calm and focused; and it helps us to do what we want to do [Shields, 2012: 117].

The techniques which can be helpful to increase the relaxation – and at the same time the resilience – are diverse and have different starting points.

One possibility is to relax the muscles. A well-known example is the progressive muscle relaxation.

With other methods we can increase the agility of the muscles. Yoga and Tai Chi can be seen as an example.

Other techniques provide the opportunity to calm the mind. The meditation is one well-known method.

Still other procedures support the internal organs so that they can beautifully modulated work. The osteopathy can be seen as an example.

To take in agents from outside can be seen as another approach to increase the relaxation and the resilience. The Western medicine, the homeopathy, etc. are well-known examples for this way.

Another course of action is to resolve energy blockades which are in the body so that the energy can flow more freely. Reiki and acupuncture can be called as two examples for this group of techniques. But also with yoga, Tai Chi, etc. it is possible to resolve energy blockades so that the different approaches do not operate independently.

We are holistic beings and all of these techniques can help us as a whole.

If we try to change our susceptibility to stress, we can assume that changes in one part have effects to (all) the other intrapersonal aspects. To relax the muscle or to increase their agility can calm the mind, can reduce negative thought patterns, etc.

These transferred effects are easily comprehensible, assuming that the different components in us interact and work more or less together. We influence other aspects with what we start and also we influence the whole system.

In a positive direction this knowledge is calming. But it is possible that a course of action has a positive effect on one aspect and a negative influence on other aspects. A local positive effect can have harmful secondary effects. Pharmaceutical products are one example for a positive potential with the risk of harmful secondary effects.

We do not know what exactly happen within us if we utilize one or more unknown interventions. We can take only a look at a part of our whole system. We – and all the other people – must focus on specific parts of our system. Over time we can broaden our point of view, but we never know how many "parts of the puzzle" exist in addition to the well-known parts.

Nobody knows what could happen in our complex system with an unknown number of transparent and non-transparent interactions; all the more the different aspects and interactions have diverse power which can be changed continuously.

In an inscrutable network with innumerable „threads“, we put one thread in vibration, and the whole network is set in motion – with developments which support the achievement of objectives, which are neutral, and which clash with positive developments.

Even if nobody has a complete comprehension about all mechanisms of action, we can broaden our point of view, if we stitch evermore "parts of the puzzle", if we prefer an eclectic approach. We have to attain a deep and wide foundation of information in combination with appropriately cognitive "governance mechanisms" which is difficult to build as a layman.

Normally, we need an expert to improve our conscious and planned individual processes significantly. It is important that the expert masters (a lot of) different techniques, methods and procedures so that he can customize the different possibilities.

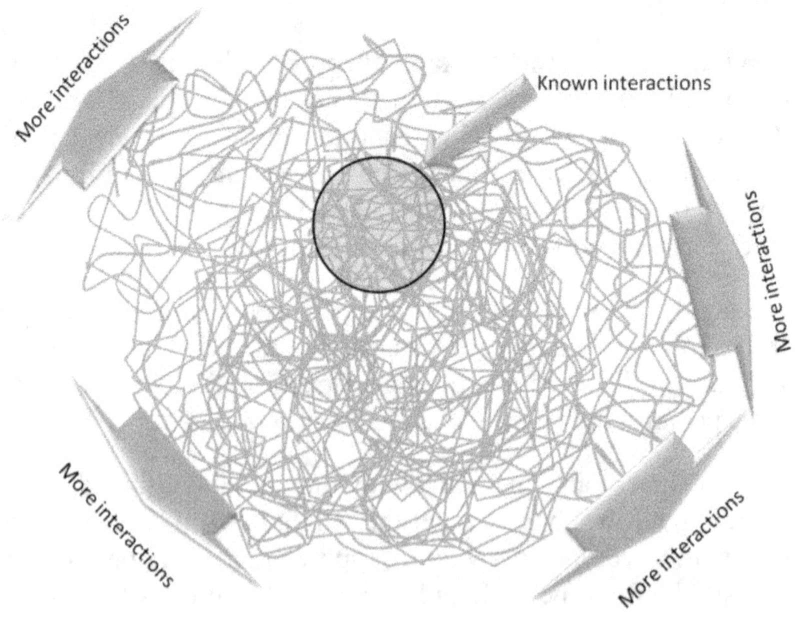

Figure 20: We know only a part of the interactions which are relevant for resilience (an illustration)

5.4 Conscious and planned processes which are managed by others

We as an individual person have to foster the ability to act in a long-run

Every expert has to realize a deep and wide foundation in his topic area. This requirement is identically equal to the requirement for social responsibility in an increasingly complex world.

Furthermore, we as experts have to optimize our intuition. It is important that we develop a "feeling" for the right intensity and frequency. It is necessary that we utilize our comprehensive potential to help others.

We are involved as a whole person – not only our mind. We have to deploy and to develop our emotions, our motivations, our attitudes, and our thoughts – and as a result we can change our activities[4].

In this context we should recognize what is really important for us, what comes to flow experiences[5], etc. If we minister to ourselves, if we do what we love, we have a great chance to support others. But we have to make sure that we do not proselytize people in our environment.

We have to minister to ourselves, and we have to concentrate on the others, with their specific needs if we try to help them. As an expert we have more power – and as a consequence thereof more social responsibility. We as experts have the responsibility

---

[4] If we change our activities alone – and not our motivations, attitudes, etc. – we run into danger to become ill during the passage of time.

[5] See for example Csikszentmihalyi & Csikszentmihalyi (1998)

to do everything in one's power to help our counterpart. Other people should trust us to act in their interest. This also includes a more neutral view on the specific problems and challenges of the other people. We as an expert are socially responsible, but not personally involved in order that we can consider the specific situation with more neutrality.

To focus only on money or other comparable benefits is not appropriate for an expert.

The extent of social responsibility is determined by subjective evaluations, because every information and experience is a "snippet" and nobody knows the totality. A comprehensive knowledge and experience is unfulfillable in a complex world. We have no frame of reference to evaluate the relevancy of the part in relation to the entirety. We can only evaluate the influence on others based on our own ethical foundation. We have to decide about the influence we have on other people; their information processing, decision making, ability to act, etc. We have to decide about our extent of social responsibility in every situation.

To develop credible decisions on a subjective level we need our intuition. We need the totality of our unconscious and conscious information processing. All of these are essential. Everybody with influence on other people needs these parts of a human being. We cannot "outsource" these important things. We cannot replace these important parts of a human by laws and other rules. We try it but without success in the long-run.

We need all our possibilities – our ethical foundation, our "feeling", our intuition, etc. – to ensure that the others around have enough freedom for an acceptable responsibility. And we should support others to carry responsibility as much as possible.

"Decentralized" responsibility on an ethical foundation reduces the burden on the shoulders of the others, so that it is important to help others to obtain or to increase their self-controlling – even if the self-controlling is reduced automatically over the years. The more people act socially responsible, the easier it is for each and every one of us.

Especially at the beginning it can be a hard "job" to support others effectively, and we have the feeling "to tilt at windmills". It is difficult to slow down the reduction of loss of control. It is a difficult undertaking but it is necessary and immutable. But in the course of time it will become better and better – we have "to stay on the ball". We can start with a "snowball" and build a big "snowman" over the years.

Those of us who can work longer with a higher social responsibility in a world with growing complexity should invest resources to help others to ensure their own self-determination (a little bit) longer.

An entrepreneur, for example, cannot concentrate on his business, he has to extend his activities – he has to encourage the self-determination, the self-controlling, the self-confidence, a perceived self-efficacy, etc. of others, too.

Bigger systems foster the ability to act in a long-run

If we support others, and if we act socially responsible, we decide what we do. A bigger system, approximately a society, can and should add another and a systematical approach: coach a lot of people systematically as an entrepreneur or as people with similar possibilities so that they can act socially responsible in a sufficient extent. This demand is necessary. And it is essential to start as fast as possible; until then enough people can act socially responsible. We need these people because social responsibility is necessary to foster it. We have to start sufficiently early, even before the problems arise.

Predictive initiatives are necessary. "To close the barn door after the horse has escaped" is the wrong approach and runs into danger of destroying the system.

Today it is mandatory to promote a great extent of individuality in an ethical framework, a deep and wide foundation of information in combination with appropriately cognitive "governance mechanisms" and a high degree of intrinsic motivation.

The support of social responsibility and its requirements should be started in the earliest babyhood, and the direct reference persons are responsible for this first support. From the beginning there is an interaction between the children and the reference persons, whereby at the beginning of life actions and reactions of children are dominantly influenced by unconscious processes[6].

If the reference persons are the parents or other relatives, we are dealing with individual persons and need their social responsibility – a good example for the necessity of a wide base in the population and an accordingly aligned education system.

Infant educators and teachers occupy a highly prioritized position. There is not hardly another position which is so important for the survival of the society as infant educators respectively

---

[6] "Childhood schooling and language come after the child's unconscious learning through experience, observation, taste, sound, smell. These are vital parts of learning culture" [Waldren, 2014: 130]. Rothbart & Bates [2006] for example go into the interaction between unconscious components and the temperament.

teachers in pre-school and in school – and maybe in exceeding phases of education.

Infant educators and teachers influence an extremely large number of people. They act as a model and often they are a reference person. They should set an example of the subjects; they have to show what children and teenagers have to learn.

For that reason it is necessary that infant educators and teachers meet very high requirements, because they have to maintain the socially responsible activities even against resistance, and they have to act socially responsible in a (highly) complex environment, so that they can foster the children and teenagers in an appropriate manner over the long term.

These requirements are not a dream. We have to realize it "now" – not in 20, 40 or 50 years. It is important to realize it before a lot of social conflicts are going to put us to an acid test. It is important to start "today", before the society is going to be overcome by the events.

To foster social responsibility has to be a very important aspect in the (pre-)school curricula – as a school subject and as an exceeding topic which is relevant in all school subjects. Social responsibility has to be omnipresent in planned and unplanned development processes.

It is no longer appropriate to fill the time in school with content-related technical subjects. Social responsibility has to be implemented as a strong conterweight. And if school cannot be integrated it in existing structures and processes, their fundamental procedure has to be changed [Hummel, 2016]. It has to reduce their content-related technical focus and it has to extend the concentration on the individuals and on their social responsibility. Comparable steps are necessary for pre-school. Here too, social responsibility has to come into focus with one of the highest priority.

Make an impact on the planned and unplanned development processes, the pressure against social responsibility is going to be far smaller as without systematic (pre-)school interventions. This is going to lead to a reduction of requirements so that more people are going to be able to act socially responsible to an appropriate extent. And it is going to lead to a lower necessity to prioritize interventions for a socially responsible mindset in the subsequent education phases (e.g. apprenticeship and the advanced vocational training).

With an outstanding support in pre-school and in school, adults can "keep trying" during their further course of their life which is much easier as to learn the relevant components in the adulthood.

Adults with a high degree of social responsibility have a high degree of self-responsibility, too. This includes that people are looking for helpful support. They are able to make use of the heteronomy in a context of a comprehensive self-determination which is embedded in responsibility.

Self-controlling and external control go hand in hand and can foster the own quality of life as well as the social success.

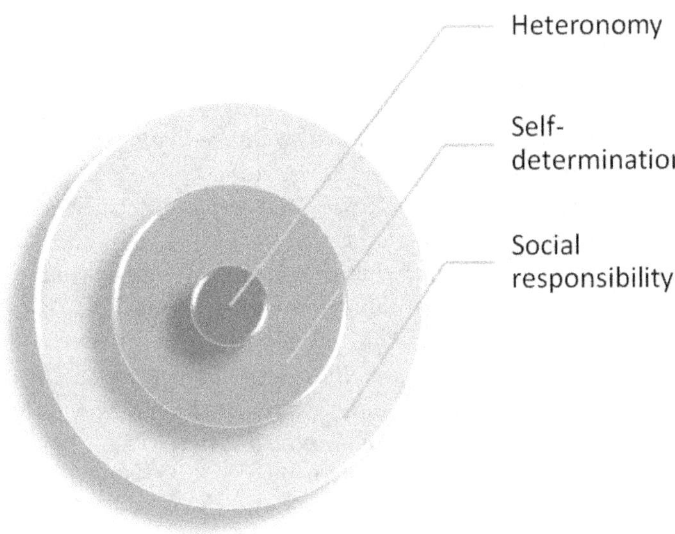

Figure 21: Heteronomy as a helpful approach in a context of self-determination embedded in social responsibility (an illustration)

Highlights:

- *All conscious activities are influenced by a vast number of unconscious processes.*
- *Our unconscious processes are very powerful with separate regulation mechanisms.*
- *Our unconscious activities can manage the conscious activities; our conscious activities can only influence most of the unconscious processes.*
- *A loss of social responsibility cannot be replaced by escalating laws and other rules. Too many rules reduce the trust and the social responsibility.*
- *Everyone has to support his own social responsibility. Curiosity, the interest in different things, resilience, etc. are equally important as mistakes and the reflection on experiences, the current situation and a possible future.*
- *We have to help others to ensure an appropriately social responsibility (a little bit) longer.*
- *It is necessary to educate people – starting in the earliest babyhood – as socially responsible citizens.*
- *Institutionalized education systems – starting in preschool – are necessary for the sustainable fitness of the society. Social responsibility must interpenetrate each fiber of the (pre-)school system.*
- *Infant educators and teachers have a highly prioritized position; no other position is so important for the survival of the society.*
- *Infant educators and teachers need comparable requirements as an entrepreneur.*

6 Conclusion

Complexity will increase continually and with a higher speed. It is a natural development process and we cannot stop it unless we destroy the system or a large part of the system.

Simultaneously a lot of us have more and more problems to manage the complex environment. It is very difficult to manage complexity, and with increasing complexity, we will be receiving evermore problems.

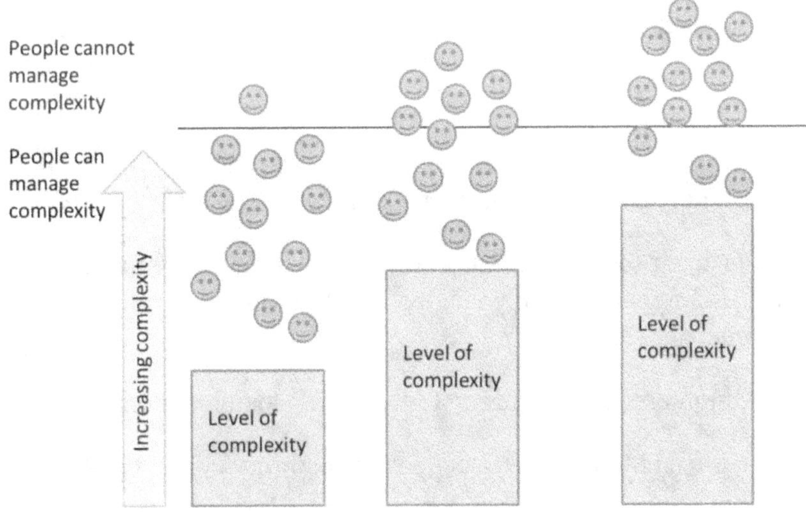

Figure 22: More and more people are unable to manage an increasing complexity (an illustration)

Without systematic interventions fewer and fewer of us have to bear a greater burden during the natural development. The burden will increase disproportionately.

Entrepreneurs, for example, become increasingly important because they are able to act suitably in a complex environment.

If we cannot manage the complexity, we cannot act socially responsible on an appropriate level. We retreat to a smaller "playing field" which is seemingly not so complex.

Our social responsibility on this smaller "playing field" works only in a (very) limited range. All the other things around are dangerous, and we are liable to fight against the "dangerous" environment, or to give up hope, become passive and ego centered.

All of us who retreat to a smaller "playing field" reduce an appropriately social responsibility in the whole system.

For each of us it is important to be able to act in a complex world as long as it is physically possible and it is important to help others accordingly.

Action ability is a cornerstone for our social responsibility.

A sufficient degree of social responsibility concerns us all.

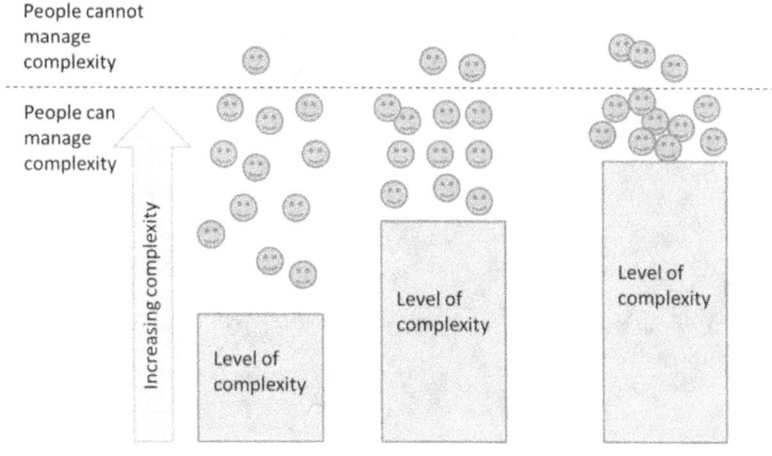

Figure 23: A lot of people have to manage higher complexity (an illustration)

Everybody who can act socially responsible has to foster overwhelmed people so that they can extend their social responsibility (active support). Simultaneously people who want support need a relief of responsibility which is possible, if others assume responsibility for them and if overwhelmed people can trust others because trust reduce the perceived complexity (passive support).

Beyond that activities systematic interventions are essential. The pre-school and the school system are two very important – and probably even the most important – institutions which can ensure the requirements to safeguard a high degree of social responsibility and the quality of human life. Social responsibility should be realized comprehensively and as fast as possible. We cannot defer indefinitely these important initiatives.

Individual and social interventions will take a long time to empower a lot of people. During the first years the interventions will have a delayed effect. A lot of staying power is necessary and further delays prolong the first signs of success superlinear.

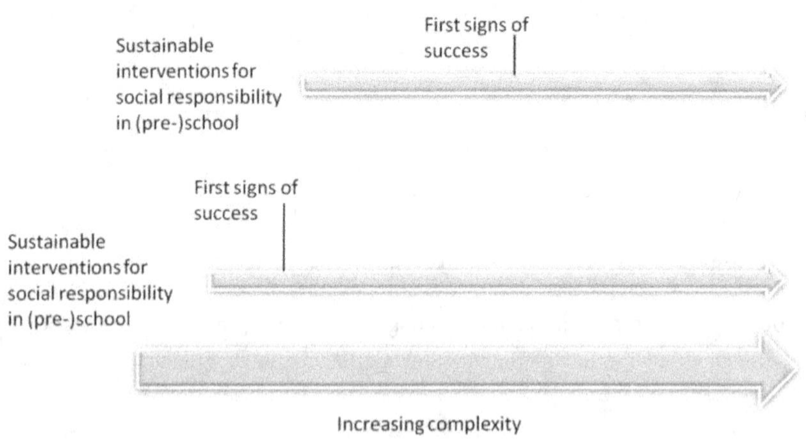

Figure 24: The later systematic interventions in (pre-)school are started; the later first signs of success are recognizable (an illustration)

Today is the right time for a great change in order that our society can survive in the future. A socially responsible majority is necessary in the future, some entrepreneurs and quite a few of us cannot maintain a big social system. A great number of "shoulders" are necessary, not fewer and fewer.

Society has to close the gap with the help of systematic interventions in pre-school and in school.

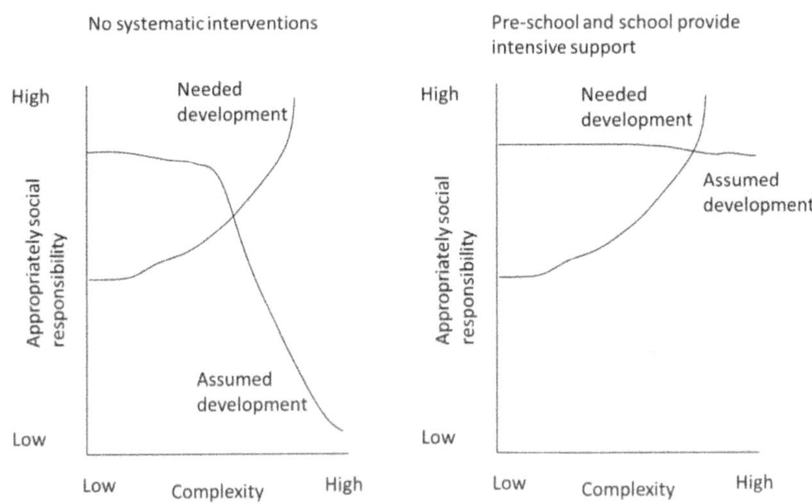

Figure 25: Threatening gap between the needed and the assumed development of social responsibility – with and without (pre-)school interventions (an illustration)

We can only hope that the policymakers and other decision makers act early enough and we, the young as well as the further generations, have the possibility to manage our / their life in the future – with a greater complexity.

All of us have the responsibility for our life and partly for the further generations. Within the framework of our possibilities and our capacity we have to act appropriately, and we have to optimize our social responsibility. We are responsible for our responsibility – each of us with his capabilities.

We do not know which concrete effects our activities bring out – in us in total and in our environment – but we can recognize which actions help us to increase our ability to act and our social responsibility.

Whatever we do, the safeguarding of the ability to act and of social responsibility are very important aspects. Only if these both components show a high score, we can ensure our quality of life for the long run. Both are not enough but they are absolutely necessary.

> **Social responsibility is too important;**
> **we have to "cosset" it.**

Comprehension Questions

1 Social responsibility as a rising challenge

1) What is the meaning of social responsibility relating to ourselves and other people?

2) In which situations do we have the responsibility for other people?

3) How are responsibility, power and freedom related to each other?

4) Why is it evermore difficult for us to assume the social responsibility for our activities?

5) What do we do, for example, if complexity outgrow us?

2 Requirements for social responsibility in a more difficult context

6) Under which conditions do we need a strong personal involvement in relation with social responsibility?

2.1 A deep and wide foundation of information

7) Why do we need a deep and wide foundation of information in the context of social responsibility?

8) Why is it often difficult to recognize if we go into too much detail?

9) Why is it positive if heuristics and other cognitive models of problem solving, decision making, etc. work unconsciously?

2.2 Intrinsic motivation

10) Why is an intrinsic motivation better than an extrinsic motivation?

2.3 Individuality

11) When is individuality important in a context of social responsibility?

12) Why are self-confidence and a perceived self-efficacy important for social responsibility?

13) Why can it be equally easy or difficult to achieve a higher degree of resilience?

3. An entrepreneur is socially responsible

14) Why is an entrepreneur predestinated for social responsibility?

15) What does the statement mean that an entrepreneur is an individualist and simultaneously social?

16) Why is it necessary for an entrepreneur to ensure an overlap with the attitudes, norms, etc. of other people?

17) Which importance does an entrepreneur have in relation to social responsibility in a world with increasing complexity?

4 Social responsibility towards the stakeholders

18) On which target group should a socially oriented business-man concentrate?

19) Why is it difficult if a businessman considers all relevant target groups?

20) What is the biggest difference between direct and indirect activities?

5.1 Individual and unconscious developments

21) Which individual aspects influence the unconscious? – Please name three examples.

22) Is it possible that cerebral activities which are unconscious improve conscious decisions? – Please give an explanation.

23) Which aspects are better to manage: unconscious or conscious activities?

5.2 Context-specific and non-transparent developments

24) Which parallels can be revealed in principle between the social development and our own conscious and unconscious activities?

25) What does coincidence or destiny mean in relation to the system specific mechanisms of self-regulation?

5.3 Individual and conscious processes

26) What do we reduce, for example, if we lose our curiosity, our interest in new discoveries, etc.?

27) What significance does the resilience have in a more and more complex environment?

28) Which possibilities help to reduce stress and foster the resilience? – Please name four examples.

5.4 Conscious and planned processes which are managed by others

29) In which development phase of a human should the support of social responsibility start?

30) Why is it so important to implement social responsibility as an essential subject in education systems?

31) Which requirements have (pre-school) teachers to fulfill if social responsibility has a high level of importance in the (pre-)school systems?

32) Why is it so important that all of us as well as social institutions help others to reinforce their social responsibility?

List of literature

Ashton, H. (2010). Undercurrents of consciousness: The endocannabinoid system. In: E. Perry, D. Collerton, F. LeBeau, & H. Ashton (eds.), *New Horizons in the Neuroscience of Consciousness*, pp. 53 – 63. Amsterdam, Philadelphia.

Balcetis, E., & Granot, Y. (2015). Under the Influence and Unaware: Unconscious Processing During Encoding, Retrieval, and Weighting in Judgment, In: G., Keren, & G. Wu (eds.), *The Wiley Blackwell Handbook of Judgment and Decision Making*, Vol. 1, pp. 333 – 355. Chichester, Malden, Oxford.

Benson, D., & Di Biase, S. A. (2015). *10 Secrets to Raising Innovative Children.* Chicago.

Blair, E. S. (2010). What you think is not what you think: unconscious and entrepreneurial behavior. In: A. A. Stanton, M. Day, & I. M. Welpe (eds.), *Neuroeconomics and the firm*, pp. 50 – 65. Cheltenham, Northampton.

Csikszentmihalyi M., & I. S. Csikszentmihalyi [eds.] (1998). *Optimal experience. Psychological studies of flow in consciousness.* Cambridge, New York, Melbourne (4th reprinted edition – First published 1988).

Glicken, M. D. (2006). *Learning from resilient people. Lessons we can apply to counseling and psychotherapy.* Thousand Oaks, London, New Delhi.

Goldstein, S., & Brooks, R. B. [eds.] (2013). *Handbook of Resilience in Children*. New York, Heidelberg, Dordrecht, London: 2th edition.

Grace, A. A. (2010). Dopamine modulation of decision making processes. In: E. Perry, D. Collerton, F. LeBeau, & H. Ashton (eds.), *New Horizons in the Neuroscience of Consciousness*, pp. 39 – 52. Amsterdam, Philadelphia.

Hummel, H.-P. (2015). *Ableitung und Konkretisierung eines ethisch fundierten Entrepreneurkonzepts. Eine interdisziplinäre Analyse*. Hamburg.

Hummel, H.-P. (2016). *Entrepreneurship Education. Von der Kita bis zum „Tod“*. Retrieved from http://bookboon.com/de/entrepreneurship-education-ebook (February 6th, 2016).

Hummel, H.-P. (2017). *Der ethisch fundierte Entrepreneur. Eine leicht verständliche Einführung*. Retrieved from http://bookboon.com/de/der-ethisch-fundierte-entrepreneur-ebook (January 5th, 2017): 2th edition.

Reich, J. W., Zautra, A. J., & Hall, J. S. [eds.] (2010). *Handbook of adult resilience*. New York, London.

Reisyan, G. D. (2013). *Neuro-Organisationskultur. Moderne Führung orientiert an Hirn- und Emotionsforschung*. Berlin, Heidelberg.

Rothbart, M. K., & Bates, J. E. (2006). Temperament. In: N. Eisenberg – Volume Editor –, W. Damon, & R. M. Lerner – Editors-in-Chief – (eds.), *Handbook of Child Psychology. Social, Emotional, and Personality Development*, Vol. 3, pp. 99 – 166. Hoboken: 6th edition.

Rüegg, J. C. (2011) . *Gehirn, Psyche und Körper. Neurobiologie von Psychosomatik und Psychotherapie.* Stuttgart: 5th updated and extended edition.

Shields, R. (2012). *Learn to relax and understand stress.* Leicester.

Taberner, K., & Taberner Siggins, K. (2015). *The power of curiosity. How to have real conversations that create collaboration, innovation and understanding.* New York.

Walde, B. (2006). Die kausale Relevanz des Mentalen – Illusion oder Realität? In: J. Reichertz, & N. Zaboura (eds.), *Akteur Gehirn – oder das vermeintliche Ende des handelnden Subjekts – Eine Kontroverse*, pp. 47 – 60. Wiesbaden.

Waldren, J. (2014). Children Negotiating Identity in Mallorca. In: J. Waldren, & I.-M. Kaminski (eds.), *Learning From The children. Childhood, Culture and Identity in a Changing World*, pp. 126 – 145. New York, Oxford.

Winters, R. W., McCabe, P. M., Green, E. J., & Schneiderman, N. (2000). Stress Responses, Coping, and Cardiovascular Neurobiology: Central Nervous System Circuitry Underlying Learned and Unlearned Affective Responses to Stressful Stimuli. In: P. M. McCabe, N. Schneiderman, F. Field, & A. R. Wellens (eds.), *Stress, Coping, and Cardiovascular Disease*, pp. 1 – 44. Mahwah.